RECEIVING THE WISDOM OF GOD

Retreat/Course Companion
WORKBOOK

RICHARD T. CASE

To my wife, Linda, who is a true partner in seeking God's wisdom together. She has a wonderful heart to hear, and to fully participate in the process of receiving God's wisdom for our life "stuff" that is personal and real to us. She knows and continues to remind me that we fundamentally do not know or have real wisdom since we are limited in understanding and do not know what is "around the corner —what is ahead in the future" that God knows. So, she encourages us to always seek God's wisdom—since such a privilege, why wouldn't we? Her insights and ideas that she brings to the process is truly such a joy to experience as we receive together God's truth and wisdom for us. I am blessed to have such a partner that stands together in this privilege—best and none better.

Acknowledgments

We wish to thank all of the leaders of our **Ministry: Living Waters—ABIDE Ministries!** These leaders fully understand seeking God's wisdom and live in this wisdom all the time. They personally assist us in confirming God's wisdom for us and for the ministry. These leaders are wonderful examples of how to seek, receive and follow God's wisdom, so that all those that come to retreats and the ones they are discipling are learning how valuable this is to be living out life on a real, practical level. Thank you all for being such true followers of Christ and His Wisdom.

These leaders are:

Jake & Mary Beckel
Joe & Leigh Bogar
Rich & Janet Cocchiaro
Larry & Sherry Collet
Scott & Kristen Cornell
David & Melissa Dunkel
Tom & Susanne Ewing
Rick & Kelly Ferris
Joel & Christina Gunn
Scott & Terry Hitchcock
Chris & Jaclyn Hoover
Rick & Nancy Hoover
Tad & Monica Jones
Ed & Becky Kobel
Don & Rachelle Light
Chris & Heidi May
Terry & Josephine Noetzel
Steve & Carolyn Van Ooteghem
Preston & Lynda Pitts
Dan & Kathy Rocconi
Bob & Keri Rockwell
John & Michelle Santaferraro
Allyson & Denny Weinberg
Neal & Kathy Weisenburger

RECEIVING THE WISDOM OF GOD: RETREAT/COURSE COMPANION WORKBOOK
PUBLISHED BY LIVING WATERS—ABIDE MINISTRIES
7615 Lemon Gulch Way
Castle Rock, CO 80108

Unless otherwise noted, all Scripture quotations are from the ESV® Bible (The Holy Bible, English Standard Version®), copyright © 2001 by Crossway Bibles, a publishing ministry of Good News Publishers. Used by permission. All rights reserved.

ISBN: 978-1-7379372-0-3
Copyright © 2024 by Richard T. Case.

All rights reserved. No part of this publication may be reproduced, distributed or transmitted in any form or by any means, including photocopying, recording, or other electronic or mechanical methods, without the prior written permission of the publisher.

Publisher's Cataloging-in-Publication data

Names:
Title:
Description: .
Identifiers: ISBN | LCCN
Subjects:

Printed in the United States of America 2024 — 2nd ed

TABLE OF CONTENTS

Introduction: 2

Lesson One:
What is Wisdom? 4

Lesson Two:
Deeper Level of Wisdom/Our Benefits 12

Lesson Three:
How Do We Receive This Wisdom 24

Lesson Four:
Experiencing the Fullness of Wisdom—The Supernatural 36

INTRODUCTION

What is your definition of "Wisdom"? and "The Supernatural"? Write the unresolved issues in your life and the questions/decisions you are facing for the uncertain times ahead. Where do you seek wisdom and God's supernatural work to bring clarity and resolution right now?

_____
_____
_____
_____
_____
_____
_____
_____
_____
_____
_____
_____
_____
_____
_____
_____
_____
_____
_____
_____

INTRODUCTION

LESSON 1:
WHAT IS WISDOM?

1. What is "wisdom?"

How do these verses define wisdom? What does that mean personally?

> **Read Proverbs 1:1-7:**
>
> The Beginning of Knowledge
> ¹ The proverbs of Solomon, son of David, king of Israel:
> ² To know wisdom and instruction,
>   to understand words of insight,
> ³ to receive instruction in wise dealing,
>   in righteousness, justice, and equity;
> ⁴ to give prudence to the simple,
>   knowledge and discretion to the youth—
> ⁵ Let the wise hear and increase in learning,
>   and the one who understands obtain guidance,
> ⁶ to understand a proverb and a saying,
>   the words of the wise and their riddles.
> ⁷ The fear of the Lord is the beginning of knowledge;
>   fools despise wisdom and instruction.

"Our role is to receive the guidance. If we're hearing it, if we're receiving it, by definition, it's because God is always giving it."

_____
_____
_____
_____
_____
_____

LESSON 1:
WHAT IS WISDOM?

What does this mean to hate evil, pride, and arrogance? How do we follow this in our everyday lives?

> **Read Proverbs 8:12-14:**
>
> ¹² "I, wisdom, dwell with prudence,
>   and I find knowledge and discretion.
> ¹³ The fear of the Lord is hatred of evil.
> Pride and arrogance and the way of evil
>   and perverted speech I hate.
> ¹⁴ I have counsel and sound wisdom;
>   I have insight; I have strength.

_____
_____
_____
_____
_____

How does this define the fear of the Lord? What does that mean personally? Why is this so important in receiving wisdom?

> **Read Proverbs 9:10-12:**
>
> ¹⁰ The fear of the Lord is the beginning of wisdom,
>   and the knowledge of the Holy One is insight.
> ¹¹ For by me your days will be multiplied,
>   and years will be added to your life.
> ¹² If you are wise, you are wise for yourself;
>   if you scoff, you alone will bear it.

LESSON 1:
WHAT IS WISDOM?

What do these verses in Exodus and Daniel tell us about wisdom? What does this mean to us in our walk of life? Why?

> **Read Exodus 35:30–36:2:**
>
> Construction of the Tabernacle
> [30] Then Moses said to the people of Israel, "See, the Lord has called by name Bezalel the son of Uri, son of Hur, of the tribe of Judah; [31] and he has filled him with the Spirit of God, with skill, with intelligence, with knowledge, and with all craftsmanship, [32] to devise artistic designs, to work in gold and silver and bronze, [33] in cutting stones for setting, and in carving wood, for work in every skilled craft. [34] And he has inspired him to teach, both him and Oholiab the son of Ahisamach of the tribe of Dan. [35] He has filled them with skill to do every sort of work done by an engraver or by a designer or by an embroiderer in blue and purple and scarlet yarns and fine twined linen, or by a weaver—by any sort of workman or skilled designer.
> [36] "Bezalel and Oholiab and every craftsman in whom the Lord has put skill and intelligence to know how to do any work in the construction of the sanctuary shall work in accordance with all that the Lord has commanded."
>
> [2] And Moses called Bezalel and Oholiab and every craftsman in whose mind the Lord had put skill, everyone whose heart stirred him up to come to do the work.

LESSON 1:
WHAT IS WISDOM?

> **Read Daniel 1:4, 17, 20:**
>
> [4] youths without blemish, of good appearance and skillful in all wisdom, endowed with knowledge, understanding learning, and competent to stand in the king's palace, and to teach them the literature and language of the Chaldeans.
>
> [17] As for these four youths, God gave them learning and skill in all literature and wisdom, and Daniel had understanding in all visions and dreams.
>
> [20] And in every matter of wisdom and understanding about which the king inquired of them, he found them ten times better than all the magicians and enchanters that were in all his kingdom.

_____
_____
_____
_____
_____

Write in journal: What elements of wisdom are particularly important to you right now? Why?

LESSON 1:
WHAT IS WISDOM?

2. **What is "wisdom" really?**

What is the difference between worldly wisdom and God's wisdom? How will we know the difference in our lives? Why is this important for us in our everyday lives?

> **Read James 3:13-18:**
>
> Wisdom from Above
> [13] Who is wise and understanding among you? By his good conduct let him show his works in the meekness of wisdom. [14] But if you have bitter jealousy and selfish ambition in your hearts, do not boast and be false to the truth. [15] This is not the wisdom that comes down from above, but is earthly, unspiritual, demonic. [16] For where jealousy and selfish ambition exist, there will be disorder and every vile practice. [17] But the wisdom from above is first pure, then peaceable, gentle, open to reason, full of mercy and good fruits, impartial and sincere. [18] And a harvest of righteousness is sown in peace by those who make peace.

_____
_____
_____
_____
_____

What wisdom did God give Daniel? On what basis did God give it? What does that mean for us and how do we receive it?

> **Read Daniel 2:20-23; 29-30:**
>
> [20] Daniel answered and said:
> "Blessed be the name of God forever and ever,
>   to whom belong wisdom and might.
> [21] He changes times and seasons;
>   he removes kings and sets up kings;
> he gives wisdom to the wise
>   and knowledge to those who have understanding;

LESSON 1:
WHAT IS WISDOM?

> ^{22} he reveals deep and hidden things;
> he knows what is in the darkness,
> and the light dwells with him.
> ^{23} To you, O God of my fathers,
> I give thanks and praise,
> for you have given me wisdom and might,
> and have now made known to me what we asked of you,
> for you have made known to us the king's matter."
>
> ^{29} To you, O king, as you lay in bed came thoughts of what would be after this, and he who reveals mysteries made known to you what is to be. ^{30} But as for me, this mystery has been revealed to me, not because of any wisdom that I have more than all the living, but in order that the interpretation may be made known to the king, and that you may know the thoughts of your mind.

_____

_____

_____

_____

What do these verses say about wisdom? Who really is wisdom, and why then is this important to us personally?

> **Read 1 Corinthians 1:21-30:**
>
> ^{21} For since, in the wisdom of God, the world did not know God through wisdom, it pleased God through the folly of what we preach[a] to save those who believe.^{22} For Jews demand signs and Greeks seek wisdom, ^{23} but we preach Christ crucified, a stumbling block to Jews and folly to Gentiles, ^{24} but to those who are called, both Jews and Greeks, Christ the power of God and the wisdom of God.^{25} For the foolishness of God is wiser than men, and the weakness of God is stronger than men.

LESSON 1:
WHAT IS WISDOM?

> ²⁶ For consider your calling, brothers: not many of you were wise according to worldly standards,[b] not many were powerful, not many were of noble birth. ²⁷ But God chose what is foolish in the world to shame the wise; God chose what is weak in the world to shame the strong; ²⁸ God chose what is low and despised in the world, even things that are not, to bring to nothing things that are, ²⁹ so that no human being[c] might boast in the presence of God. ³⁰ And because of him[d] you are in Christ Jesus, who became to us wisdom from God, righteousness and sanctification and redemption,

_____
_____
_____
_____
_____

Knowing that Christ is wisdom and that He gives wisdom to us, what do these verses tell us that are important to our lives? Why?

> **Read Colossians 2:1-3; 9-10:**
>
> **2** For I want you to know how great a struggle I have for you and for those at Laodicea and for all who have not seen me face to face, ² that their hearts may be encouraged, being knit together in love, to reach all the riches of full assurance of understanding and the knowledge of God's mystery, which is Christ, ³ in whom are hidden all the treasures of wisdom and knowledge.
>
> ⁹ For in him the whole fullness of deity dwells bodily, ¹⁰ and you have been filled in him, who is the head of all rule and authority.

_____
_____
_____
_____
_____

LESSON 1:
WHAT IS WISDOM?

What do these verses say about the Spirit of wisdom? What is the difference between spiritual wisdom and worldly (natural) wisdom? Why is this so important for us in our lives?

> **Read Isaiah 11:1-3:**
>
> The Righteous Reign of the Branch
> **11** There shall come forth a shoot from the stump of Jesse,
>   and a branch from his roots shall bear fruit.
> ² And the Spirit of the Lord shall rest upon him,
>   the Spirit of wisdom and understanding,
>   the Spirit of counsel and might,
>   the Spirit of knowledge and the fear of the Lord.
> ³ And his delight shall be in the fear of the Lord.
> He shall not judge by what his eyes see,
>   or decide disputes by what his ears hear,

_____
_____
_____
_____
_____

Write in journal: What characteristics of Christ as "The" Wisdom of God are meaningful to you? Why?

LESSON 2:
DEEPER LEVEL OF WISDOM/OUR BENEFITS

3. **What is the deeper level of wisdom (discernment)?**

What are all these qualities of wisdom that provide us the privilege of walking on His wonderful path for our lives? What do they mean for us personally?

> **Read Psalm 19:7-14:**
>
> [7] The law of the Lord is perfect,[a]
>   reviving the soul;
> the testimony of the Lord is sure,
>   making wise the simple;
> [8] the precepts of the Lord are right,
>   rejoicing the heart;
> the commandment of the Lord is pure,
>   enlightening the eyes;
> [9] the fear of the Lord is clean,
>   enduring forever;
> the rules[b] of the Lord are true,
>   and righteous altogether.
> [10] More to be desired are they than gold,
>   even much fine gold;
> sweeter also than honey
>   and drippings of the honeycomb.
> [11] Moreover, by them is your servant warned;
>   in keeping them there is great reward.
> [12] Who can discern his errors?
>   Declare me innocent from hidden faults.
> [13] Keep back your servant also from presumptuous sins;
>   let them not have dominion over me!
> Then I shall be blameless,
>   and innocent of great transgression.
> [14] Let the words of my mouth and the meditation of my heart
>   be acceptable in your sight,
>   O Lord, my rock and my redeemer.

"We will know with certainty what He is revealing to us, so we walk on His path, which is best and none better, all for our benefit."

LESSON 2:
DEEPER LEVEL OF WISDOM/OUR BENEFITS

_____
_____
_____
_____
_____

What is the key to being transformed and proving out His will? Why is that important and how do we practically live this out?

> **Read Romans 12:1-2:**
>
> A Living Sacrifice
> **12** I appeal to you therefore, brothers,[a] by the mercies of God, to present your bodies as a living sacrifice, holy and acceptable to God, which is your spiritual worship.[b] 2 Do not be conformed to this world,[c] but be transformed by the renewal of your mind, that by testing you may discern what is the will of God, what is good and acceptable and perfect.[d]

_____
_____
_____
_____

LESSON 2:
DEEPER LEVEL OF WISDOM/OUR BENEFITS

In these verses, how does this spiritual process work? What does it mean for us to receive His wisdom? How do we live this out practically in our life?

> **Read 1 Corinthians 2:9-16:**
>
> 9 But, as it is written,
> "What no eye has seen, nor ear heard,
>   nor the heart of man imagined,
> what God has prepared for those who love him"—
> 10 these things God has revealed to us through the Spirit. For the Spirit searches everything, even the depths of God. 11 For who knows a person's thoughts except the spirit of that person, which is in him? So also no one comprehends the thoughts of God except the Spirit of God. 12 Now we have received not the spirit of the world, but the Spirit who is from God, that we might understand the things freely given us by God. 13 And we impart this in words not taught by human wisdom but taught by the Spirit, interpreting spiritual truths to those who are spiritual.[a]
>
> 14 The natural person does not accept the things of the Spirit of God, for they are folly to him, and he is not able to understand them because they are spiritually discerned. 15 The spiritual person judges all things, but is himself to be judged by no one. 16 "For who has understood the mind of the Lord so as to instruct him?" But we have the mind of Christ.

_____
_____
_____
_____
_____

LESSON 2:
DEEPER LEVEL OF WISDOM/OUR BENEFITS

What do these verses say is real wisdom? Why is this necessary to live our lives according to God's will?

> **Read 1 Kings 3:5-9:**
>
> ⁵ At Gibeon the Lord appeared to Solomon in a dream by night, and God said, "Ask what I shall give you." ⁶ And Solomon said, "You have shown great and steadfast love to your servant David my father, because he walked before you in faithfulness, in righteousness, and in uprightness of heart toward you. And you have kept for him this great and steadfast love and have given him a son to sit on his throne this day. ⁷ And now, O Lord my God, you have made your servant king in place of David my father, although I am but a little child. I do not know how to go out or come in. ⁸ And your servant is in the midst of your people whom you have chosen, a great people, too many to be numbered or counted for multitude. ⁹ Give your servant therefore an understanding mind to govern your people, that I may discern between good and evil, for who is able to govern this your great people?"

_____
_____
_____
_____
_____

LESSON 2:
DEEPER LEVEL OF WISDOM/OUR BENEFITS

What does this story tell us happened to Joseph regarding his receiving wisdom and how it impacted him? Why is this important to us and how we live our everyday lives?

Read Genesis 41:1-56:

Joseph Interprets Pharaoh's Dreams
41 After two whole years, Pharaoh dreamed that he was standing by the Nile, 2 and behold, there came up out of the Nile seven cows, attractive and plump, and they fed in the reed grass. 3 And behold, seven other cows, ugly and thin, came up out of the Nile after them, and stood by the other cows on the bank of the Nile. 4 And the ugly, thin cows ate up the seven attractive, plump cows. And Pharaoh awoke. 5 And he fell asleep and dreamed a second time. And behold, seven ears of grain, plump and good, were growing on one stalk. 6 And behold, after them sprouted seven ears, thin and blighted by the east wind. 7 And the thin ears swallowed up the seven plump, full ears. And Pharaoh awoke, and behold, it was a dream. 8 So in the morning his spirit was troubled, and he sent and called for all the magicians of Egypt and all its wise men. Pharaoh told them his dreams, but there was none who could interpret them to Pharaoh.

9 Then the chief cupbearer said to Pharaoh, "I remember my offenses today. 10 When Pharaoh was angry with his servants and put me and the chief baker in custody in the house of the captain of the guard, 11 we dreamed on the same night, he and I, each having a dream with its own interpretation. 12 A young Hebrew was there with us, a servant of the captain of the guard. When we told him, he interpreted our dreams to us, giving an interpretation to each man according to his dream. 13 And as he interpreted to us, so it came about. I was restored to my office, and the baker was hanged."
14 Then Pharaoh sent and called Joseph, and they quickly brought him out of the pit. And when he had shaved himself and changed his clothes, he came in before Pharaoh. 15 And Pharaoh said to Joseph, "I have had a dream, and there is no one who can interpret it. I have heard it said of you that when you hear a dream you can interpret it." 16 Joseph answered Pharaoh, "It is not in me; God will give Pharaoh a favorable answer."[a] 17 Then Pharaoh said to Joseph, "Behold, in my dream I was standing on the banks of the Nile. 18 Seven cows, plump and attractive, came up out of the Nile and fed in the reed grass. 19 Seven other

LESSON 2:
DEEPER LEVEL OF WISDOM/OUR BENEFITS

cows came up after them, poor and very ugly and thin, such as I had never seen in all the land of Egypt. 20 And the thin, ugly cows ate up the first seven plump cows,21 but when they had eaten them no one would have known that they had eaten them, for they were still as ugly as at the beginning. Then I awoke. 22 I also saw in my dream seven ears growing on one stalk, full and good. 23 Seven ears, withered, thin, and blighted by the east wind, sprouted after them, 24 and the thin ears swallowed up the seven good ears. And I told it to the magicians, but there was no one who could explain it to me."

25 Then Joseph said to Pharaoh, "The dreams of Pharaoh are one; God has revealed to Pharaoh what he is about to do. 26 The seven good cows are seven years, and the seven good ears are seven years; the dreams are one. 27 The seven lean and ugly cows that came up after them are seven years, and the seven empty ears blighted by the east wind are also seven years of famine. 28 It is as I told Pharaoh; God has shown to Pharaoh what he is about to do. 29 There will come seven years of great plenty throughout all the land of Egypt, 30 but after them there will arise seven years of famine, and all the plenty will be forgotten in the land of Egypt. The famine will consume the land, 31 and the plenty will be unknown in the land by reason of the famine that will follow, for it will be very severe. 32 And the doubling of Pharaoh's dream means that the thing is fixed by God, and God will shortly bring it about. 33 Now therefore let Pharaoh select a discerning and wise man, and set him over the land of Egypt. 34 Let Pharaoh proceed to appoint overseers over the land and take one-fifth of the produce of the land[b] of Egypt during the seven plentiful years. 35 And let them gather all the food of these good years that are coming and store up grain under the authority of Pharaoh for food in the cities, and let them keep it. 36 That food shall be a reserve for the land against the seven years of famine that are to occur in the land of Egypt, so that the land may not perish through the famine."
Joseph Rises to Power

37 This proposal pleased Pharaoh and all his servants. 38 And Pharaoh said to his servants, "Can we find a man like this, in whom is the Spirit of God?"[c] 39 Then Pharaoh said to Joseph, "Since God has shown you all this, there is none so discerning and wise as you are. 40 You shall be over my house, and all my people shall order themselves as you command.[d] Only as regards the throne will I be greater than you." 41 And Pharaoh said to Joseph, "See, I have set you over all the land of Egypt." 42 Then Pharaoh took his signet ring from his hand and put

LESSON 2:
DEEPER LEVEL OF WISDOM/OUR BENEFITS

it on Joseph's hand, and clothed him in garments of fine linen and put a gold chain about his neck. 43 And he made him ride in his second chariot. And they called out before him, "Bow the knee!"[e] Thus he set him over all the land of Egypt. 44 Moreover, Pharaoh said to Joseph, "I am Pharaoh, and without your consent no one shall lift up hand or foot in all the land of Egypt." 45 And Pharaoh called Joseph's name Zaphenath-paneah. And he gave him in marriage Asenath, the daughter of Potiphera priest of On. So Joseph went out over the land of Egypt.

46 Joseph was thirty years old when he entered the service of Pharaoh king of Egypt. And Joseph went out from the presence of Pharaoh and went through all the land of Egypt. 47 During the seven plentiful years the earth produced abundantly, 48 and he gathered up all the food of these seven years, which occurred in the land of Egypt, and put the food in the cities. He put in every city the food from the fields around it. 49 And Joseph stored up grain in great abundance, like the sand of the sea, until he ceased to measure it, for it could not be measured.

50 Before the year of famine came, two sons were born to Joseph. Asenath, the daughter of Potiphera priest of On, bore them to him. 51 Joseph called the name of the firstborn Manasseh. "For," he said, "God has made me forget all my hardship and all my father's house."[f] 52 The name of the second he called Ephraim, "For God has made me fruitful in the land of my affliction."[g]
53 The seven years of plenty that occurred in the land of Egypt came to an end, 54 and the seven years of famine began to come, as Joseph had said. There was famine in all lands, but in all the land of Egypt there was bread. 55 When all the land of Egypt was famished, the people cried to Pharaoh for bread. Pharaoh said to all the Egyptians, "Go to Joseph. What he says to you, do."

56 So when the famine had spread over all the land, Joseph opened all the storehouses[h] and sold to the Egyptians, for the famine was severe in the land of Egypt.

_____
_____
_____
_____
_____

LESSON 2:
DEEPER LEVEL OF WISDOM/OUR BENEFITS

What does this tell us happens when we talk to one another? How is this such a wonderful process for us to receive God's wisdom? How then should we process things together to receive God's wisdom? Why?

> **Read Malachi 3:16-18:**
>
> The Book of Remembrance
> [16] Then those who feared the Lord spoke with one another. The Lord paid attention and heard them, and a book of remembrance was written before him of those who feared the Lord and esteemed his name. [17] "They shall be mine, says the Lord of hosts, in the day when I make up my treasured possession, and I will spare them as a man spares his son who serves him. [18] Then once more you shall see the distinction between the righteous and the wicked, between one who serves God and one who does not serve him.

_____
_____
_____
_____
_____

Write in journal: Regarding your issues and questions: What discernment are you receiving that helps you understand the truth and thus God's will better?

4.   What are the benefits of this wisdom to us?

What do these verses list as benefits to receiving wisdom? How might we apply these to our everyday lives?

> **Read Proverbs 3:13-18:**
>
> Blessed Is the One Who Finds Wisdom
> [13] Blessed is the one who finds wisdom,
>   and the one who gets understanding,
> [14] for the gain from her is better than gain from silver

LESSON 2:
DEEPER LEVEL OF WISDOM/OUR BENEFITS

> and her profit better than gold.
> ¹⁵ She is more precious than jewels,
>   and nothing you desire can compare with her.
> ¹⁶ Long life is in her right hand;
>   in her left hand are riches and honor.
> ¹⁷ Her ways are ways of pleasantness,
>   and all her paths are peace.
> ¹⁸ She is a tree of life to those who lay hold of her;
>   those who hold her fast are called blessed.

_____
_____
_____
_____
_____

By walking in wisdom, who is the recipient of wisdom? What does this mean, and why is this important?

> **Read Proverbs 9:10-12:**
>
> ¹⁰ The fear of the Lord is the beginning of wisdom,
>   and the knowledge of the Holy One is insight.
> ¹¹ For by me your days will be multiplied,
>   and years will be added to your life.
> ¹² If you are wise, you are wise for yourself;
>   if you scoff, you alone will bear it.

_____
_____
_____
_____
_____

LESSON 2:
DEEPER LEVEL OF WISDOM/OUR BENEFITS

As we live in His wisdom, what does that do for us? How important is that for living a life of stability and security? Why?

> **Read Proverbs 14:26-27:**
>
> 26 In the fear of the Lord one has strong confidence,
>   and his children will have a refuge.
> 27 The fear of the Lord is a fountain of life,
>   that one may turn away from the snares of death.

_____
_____
_____
_____
_____

If we live in wisdom, what follows us? Why is that such a wonderful place to live?

> **Read Proverbs 16:20-21:**
>
> 20 Whoever gives thought to the word[a] will discover good,
>   and blessed is he who trusts in the Lord.
> 21 The wise of heart is called discerning,
>   and sweetness of speech increases persuasiveness.

_____
_____
_____
_____
_____

LESSON 2:
DEEPER LEVEL OF WISDOM/OUR BENEFITS

With wisdom, what will we live in and not experience? What does that mean to us in our lives, personally?

> **Read Proverbs 19:8; 23:**
>
> ⁸ Whoever gets sense loves his own soul;
>   he who keeps understanding will discover good.
>
> ²³ The fear of the Lord leads to life,
>   and whoever has it rests satisfied;
>   he will not be visited by harm.

_____
_____
_____
_____
_____

What in these verses are all the benefits listed of receiving wisdom? What do these mean to us in our everyday lives?

> **Read Proverbs 2:5-10:**
>
> ⁵ then you will understand the fear of the Lord
>   and find the knowledge of God.
> ⁶ For the Lord gives wisdom;
>   from his mouth come knowledge and understanding;
> ⁷ he stores up sound wisdom for the upright;
>   he is a shield to those who walk in integrity,
> ⁸ guarding the paths of justice
>   and watching over the way of his saints.
> ⁹ Then you will understand righteousness and justice
>   and equity, every good path;
> ¹⁰ for wisdom will come into your heart,
>   and knowledge will be pleasant to your soul;

LESSON 2:
DEEPER LEVEL OF WISDOM/OUR BENEFITS

_____
_____
_____
_____
_____

Write in journal: What benefits have you recently experienced? How? What benefits have you not recently experienced? Why?

LESSON 3:
HOW DO WE RECEIVE THIS WISDOM?

5. How do we receive this wisdom?

What are the two keys to receiving wisdom, as Solomon asked for? What does that look like in our personal life?

> **Read 1 Kings 3:3-14:**
>
> **3** Solomon loved the Lord, walking in the statutes of David his father, only he sacrificed and made offerings at the high places. ⁴ And the king went to Gibeon to sacrifice there, for that was the great high place. Solomon used to offer a thousand burnt offerings on that altar. ⁵ At Gibeon the Lord appeared to Solomon in a dream by night, and God said, "Ask what I shall give you." ⁶ And Solomon said, "You have shown great and steadfast love to your servant David my father, because he walked before you in faithfulness, in righteousness, and in uprightness of heart toward you. And you have kept for him this great and steadfast love and have given him a son to sit on his throne this day. ⁷ And now, O Lord my God, you have made your servant king in place of David my father, although I am but a little child. I do not know how to go out or come in. ⁸ And your servant is in the midst of your people whom you have chosen, a great people, too many to be numbered or counted for multitude. ⁹ Give your servant therefore an understanding mind to govern your people, that I may discern between good and evil, for who is able to govern this your great people?"
>
> ¹⁰ It pleased the Lord that Solomon had asked this. ¹¹ And God said to him, "Because you have asked this, and have not asked for yourself long life or riches or the life of your enemies, but have asked for yourself understanding to discern what is right, ¹² behold, I now do according to your word. Behold, I give you a wise and discerning mind, so that none like you has been before you and none like you shall arise after you. ¹³ I

> "We need that discernment that is spiritual and not logical. We will need the ability to increase our sensitivity, and the ability to hear better. This is what is needed and what we should pray for."

LESSON 3:
HOW DO WE RECEIVE THIS WISDOM?

> give you also what you have not asked, both riches and honor, so that no other king shall compare with you, all your days. [14] And if you will walk in my ways, keeping my statutes and my commandments, as your father David walked, then I will lengthen your days."

_____
_____
_____
_____

What does David say is important for him to receive wisdom? What does that look like for each of us personally?

> **Read Psalm 51:16-19:**
>
> [16] For you will not delight in sacrifice, or I would give it;
>   you will not be pleased with a burnt offering.
> [17] The sacrifices of God are a broken spirit;
>   a broken and contrite heart, O God, you will not despise.
> [18] Do good to Zion in your good pleasure;
>   build up the walls of Jerusalem;
> [19] then will you delight in right sacrifices,
>   in burnt offerings and whole burnt offerings;
>   then bulls will be offered on your altar.

_____
_____
_____
_____

LESSON 3:
HOW DO WE RECEIVE THIS WISDOM?

What do these verses say about Solomon's heart? What does that mean and how do we apply this to our lives?

> **Read 1 Kings 4:29-30:**
>
> ²⁹ And God gave Solomon wisdom and understanding beyond measure, and breadth of mind like the sand on the seashore, ³⁰ so that Solomon's wisdom surpassed the wisdom of all the people of the east and all the wisdom of Egypt.

_____
_____
_____
_____
_____

What happened when the Queen of Sheba came and visited Solomon? How do we receive this regarding God giving us wisdom and applying this to our lives?

> **Read 2 Chronicles 9:1-12; 22-23:**
>
> The Queen of Sheba
> **9** Now when the queen of Sheba heard of the fame of Solomon, she came to Jerusalem to test him with hard questions, having a very great retinue and camels bearing spices and very much gold and precious stones. And when she came to Solomon, she told him all that was on her mind. ² And Solomon answered all her questions. There was nothing hidden from Solomon that he could not explain to her. ³ And when the queen of Sheba had seen the wisdom of Solomon, the house that he had built, ⁴ the food of his table, the seating of his officials, and the attendance of his servants, and their clothing, his cupbearers, and their clothing, and his burnt offerings that he offered at the house of the Lord, there was no more breath in her.

LESSON 3:
HOW DO WE RECEIVE THIS WISDOM?

> [5] And she said to the king, "The report was true that I heard in my own land of your words and of your wisdom, [6] but I did not believe the[a] reports until I came and my own eyes had seen it. And behold, half the greatness of your wisdom was not told me; you surpass the report that I heard. [7] Happy are your wives![b] Happy are these your servants, who continually stand before you and hear your wisdom! 8 Blessed be the Lord your God, who has delighted in you and set you on his throne as king for the Lord your God! Because your God loved Israel and would establish them forever, he has made you king over them, that you may execute justice and righteousness." [9] Then she gave the king 120 talents[c] of gold, and a very great quantity of spices, and precious stones. There were no spices such as those that the queen of Sheba gave to King Solomon.
>
> [10] Moreover, the servants of Hiram and the servants of Solomon, who brought gold from Ophir, brought algum wood and precious stones. [11] And the king made from the algum wood supports for the house of the Lord and for the king's house, lyres also and harps for the singers. There never was seen the like of them before in the land of Judah.
>
> [12] And King Solomon gave to the queen of Sheba all that she desired, whatever she asked besides what she had brought to the king. So she turned and went back to her own land with her servants.

_____
_____
_____
_____
_____

LESSON 3:
HOW DO WE RECEIVE THIS WISDOM?

What are the activities that are our responsibilities as we pursue wisdom? What do these look like in our lives?

> **Read Proverbs 2:1-4:**
>
> The Value of Wisdom
> **2** My son, if you receive my words
>   and treasure up my commandments with you,
> ² making your ear attentive to wisdom
>   and inclining your heart to understanding;
> ³ yes, if you call out for insight
>   and raise your voice for understanding,
> ⁴ if you seek it like silver
>   and search for it as for hidden treasures,

_____
_____
_____
_____
_____

As we are receiving wisdom, what is important for us to receive it? How do we apply this in our everyday lives?

> **Read Proverbs 4:1-9; 20-23:**
>
> A Father's Wise Instruction
> **4** Hear, O sons, a father's instruction,
>   and be attentive, that you may gain[a] insight,
> ² for I give you good precepts;
>   do not forsake my teaching.
> ³ When I was a son with my father,
>   tender, the only one in the sight of my mother,
> ⁴ he taught me and said to me,
> "Let your heart hold fast my words;

LESSON 3:
HOW DO WE RECEIVE THIS WISDOM?

>   keep my commandments, and live.
> 5 Get wisdom; get insight;
>   do not forget, and do not turn away from the words of my mouth.
> 6 Do not forsake her, and she will keep you;
>   love her, and she will guard you.
> 7 The beginning of wisdom is this: Get wisdom,
>   and whatever you get, get insight.
> 8 Prize her highly, and she will exalt you;
>   she will honor you if you embrace her.
> 9 She will place on your head a graceful garland;
>   she will bestow on you a beautiful crown."
>
> 20 My son, be attentive to my words;
>   incline your ear to my sayings.
> 21 Let them not escape from your sight;
>   keep them within your heart.
> 22 For they are life to those who find them,
>   and healing to all their[a] flesh.
> 23 Keep your heart with all vigilance,
>   for from it flow the springs of life.

_____
_____
_____
_____
_____

LESSON 3:
HOW DO WE RECEIVE THIS WISDOM?

As we are paying attention, what are the three things we are to do to receive the answers? What does that look like in our everyday lives?

> **Read Proverbs 8:32-35:**
>
> ³² "And now, O sons, listen to me:
>   blessed are those who keep my ways.
> ³³ Hear instruction and be wise,
>   and do not neglect it.
> ³⁴ Blessed is the one who listens to me,
>   watching daily at my gates,
>   waiting beside my doors.
> ³⁵ For whoever finds me finds life
>   and obtains favor from the Lord,

_____
_____
_____
_____
_____

> **Read Proverbs 11:14; 15:22:**
>
> ¹⁴ Where there is no guidance, a people falls,
>   but in an abundance of counselors there is safety.
>
> ²² Without counsel plans fail,
>   but with many advisers they succeed.

_____
_____
_____
_____
_____

LESSON 3:
HOW DO WE RECEIVE THIS WISDOM?

Since receiving wisdom is a spiritual process, how does this spiritual process work? How do we apply this to our lives?

> **Read 1 Corinthians 2:9-12:**
>
> ⁹ But, as it is written,
> "What no eye has seen, nor ear heard,
>   nor the heart of man imagined,
> what God has prepared for those who love him"—
> ¹⁰ these things God has revealed to us through the Spirit. For the Spirit searches everything, even the depths of God. ¹¹ For who knows a person's thoughts except the spirit of that person, which is in him? So also no one comprehends the thoughts of God except the Spirit of God. ¹² Now we have received not the spirit of the world, but the Spirit who is from God, that we might understand the things freely given us by God.

_____
_____
_____
_____
_____

In seeking wisdom, what are we to do and have settled in order for us to receive it? What does this mean to us personally?

> **Read James 1:5-8:**
> ⁵ If any of you lacks wisdom, let him ask God, who gives generously to all without reproach, and it will be given him. ⁶ But let him ask in faith, with no doubting, for the one who doubts is like a wave of the sea that is driven and tossed by the wind. ⁷ For that person must not suppose that he will receive anything from the Lord; ⁸ he is a double-minded man, unstable in all his ways.

LESSON 3:
HOW DO WE RECEIVE THIS WISDOM?

_____
_____
_____
_____
_____

In these verses, what is our prayer as we seek wisdom? What does all this mean to us personally?

> **Read Ephesians 1:16-21:**
>
> [16] I do not cease to give thanks for you, remembering you in my prayers, [17] that the God of our Lord Jesus Christ, the Father of glory, may give you the Spirit of wisdom and of revelation in the knowledge of him, [18] having the eyes of your hearts enlightened, that you may know what is the hope to which he has called you, what are the riches of his glorious inheritance in the saints, [19] and what is the immeasurable greatness of his power toward us who believe, according to the working of his great might [20] that he worked in Christ when he raised him from the dead and seated him at his right hand in the heavenly places, [21] far above all rule and authority and power and dominion, and above every name that is named, not only in this age but also in the one to come.

_____
_____
_____
_____
_____

LESSON 3:
HOW DO WE RECEIVE THIS WISDOM?

What else are we to pray? How does this apply to our lives?

> **Read Colossians 1: 9-12:**
>
> [9] And so, from the day we heard, we have not ceased to pray for you, asking that you may be filled with the knowledge of his will in all spiritual wisdom and understanding, [10] so as to walk in a manner worthy of the Lord, fully pleasing to him: bearing fruit in every good work and increasing in the knowledge of God; [11] being strengthened with all power, according to his glorious might, for all endurance and patience with joy; [12] giving thanks[a] to the Father, who has qualified you[b] to share in the inheritance of the saints in light.

_____
_____
_____
_____

As we receive wisdom, what does He tell us is a quality that helps reach confirmation? How does this work in our everyday decision making?

> **Read Colossians 3:12-17:**
>
> [12] Put on then, as God's chosen ones, holy and beloved, compassionate hearts, kindness, humility, meekness, and patience, [13] bearing with one another and, if one has a complaint against another, forgiving each other; as the Lord has forgiven you, so you also must forgive. [14] And above all these put on love, which binds everything together in perfect harmony. [15] And let the peace of Christ rule in your hearts, to which indeed you were called in one body. And be thankful. [16] Let the word of Christ dwell in you richly, teaching and admonishing one another in all wisdom, singing psalms and hymns and spiritual songs, with thankfulness in your hearts to God. [17] And whatever you do, in word or deed, do everything in the name of the Lord Jesus, giving thanks to God the Father through him.

LESSON 3:
HOW DO WE RECEIVE THIS WISDOM?

_____
_____
_____
_____
_____

What do these verses tell us about how we apply wisdom? What does this look like in our everyday lives?

> **Read Colossians 4:2-6:**
>
> Further Instructions
> ² Continue steadfastly in prayer, being watchful in it with thanksgiving. ³ At the same time, pray also for us, that God may open to us a door for the word, to declare the mystery of Christ, on account of which I am in prison— ⁴ that I may make it clear, which is how I ought to speak.
>
> ⁵ Walk in wisdom toward outsiders, making the best use of the time. 6 Let your speech always be gracious, seasoned with salt, so that you may know how you ought to answer each person.

_____
_____
_____
_____
_____

LESSON 3:
HOW DO WE RECEIVE THIS WISDOM?

Write in journal: What is God inviting you to consider in strengthening your ability to receive wisdom from Him? Go back over your list of questions/unresolved issues for which you seek wisdom (from introductory exercise) and pray together for wisdom from God.

LESSON 4:
EXPERIENCING THE FULLNESS OF WISDOM—THE SUPERNATURAL

6. **Experiencing the Supernatural (Power; Prophetic; Miraculous).**

As God gives us wisdom, what should we expect? What does this mean to us personally?

> **Read 1 Corinthians 2:1-5:**
>
> Proclaiming Christ Crucified
> **2** And I, when I came to you, brothers,[a] did not come proclaiming to you the testimony[b] of God with lofty speech or wisdom. ² For I decided to know nothing among you except Jesus Christ and him crucified. ³ And I was with you in weakness and in fear and much trembling, ⁴ and my speech and my message were not in plausible words of wisdom, but in demonstration of the Spirit and of power, ⁵ so that your faith might not rest in the wisdom of men[c] but in the power of God.

> "Wisdom is getting us in the right place at the right time with the right people so that He can fulfill His power."

_____
_____
_____
_____
_____

LESSON 4:
EXPERIENCING THE FULLNESS OF WISDOM—THE SUPERNATURAL

What does God say about Him bearing witness to such a great salvation that we are to experience? Why? What can we then expect in our lives?

> **Read Hebrews 2:1-4**
>
> Warning Against Neglecting Salvation
> **2** Therefore we must pay much closer attention to what we have heard, lest we drift away from it. ² For since the message declared by angels proved to be reliable, and every transgression or disobedience received a just retribution,³ how shall we escape if we neglect such a great salvation? It was declared at first by the Lord, and it was attested to us by those who heard, ⁴ while God also bore witness by signs and wonders and various miracles and by gifts of the Holy Spirit distributed according to his will.

_____
_____
_____
_____

What are these gifts of the Holy Spirit? How are they manifested through us, and what does that mean in our lives?

> **Read 1 Corinthians 12:1-11:**
>
> Spiritual Gifts
> **12** Now concerning[a] spiritual gifts,[b] brothers,[c] I do not want you to be uninformed. ² You know that when you were pagans you were led astray to mute idols, however you were led. ³ Therefore I want you to understand that no one speaking in the Spirit of God ever says "Jesus is accursed!" and no one can say "Jesus is Lord" except in the Holy Spirit.

LESSON 4:
EXPERIENCING THE FULLNESS OF WISDOM—THE SUPERNATURAL

> 4 Now there are varieties of gifts, but the same Spirit; 5 and there are varieties of service, but the same Lord; 6 and there are varieties of activities, but it is the same God who empowers them all in everyone. 7 To each is given the manifestation of the Spirit for the common good. 8 For to one is given through the Spirit the utterance of wisdom, and to another the utterance of knowledge according to the same Spirit, 9 to another faith by the same Spirit, to another gifts of healing by the one Spirit, 10 to another the working of miracles, to another prophecy, to another the ability to distinguish between spirits, to another various kinds of tongues, to another the interpretation of tongues. 11 All these are empowered by one and the same Spirit, who apportions to each one individually as he wills.

_____
_____
_____
_____
_____

7. How do we Experience this Supernatural Work in our real lives with "Christ in us?"

As we read these stories, what are the keys to experiencing the supernatural work of God as we walk in wisdom? How will these be experienced by us in our lives?

> **Read Matthew 8:1-13; 23- 27:**
>
> Jesus Cleanses a Leper
> **8** When he came down from the mountain, great crowds followed him. 2 And behold, a leper[a] came to him and knelt before him, saying, "Lord, if you will, you can make me clean." 3 And Jesus[b] stretched out his hand and touched him, saying, "I will; be clean." And immediately his leprosy was cleansed. 4 And Jesus said to him, "See that you say nothing to anyone, but go, show yourself to the priest and offer the gift that Moses commanded, for a proof to them."

LESSON 4:
EXPERIENCING THE FULLNESS OF WISDOM—THE SUPERNATURAL

The Faith of a Centurion

5 When he had entered Capernaum, a centurion came forward to him, appealing to him, 6 "Lord, my servant is lying paralyzed at home, suffering terribly." 7 And he said to him, "I will come and heal him." 8 But the centurion replied, "Lord, I am not worthy to have you come under my roof, but only say the word, and my servant will be healed. 9 For I too am a man under authority, with soldiers under me. And I say to one, 'Go,' and he goes, and to another, 'Come,' and he comes, and to my servant,[c] 'Do this,' and he does it." 10 When Jesus heard this, he marveled and said to those who followed him, "Truly, I tell you, with no one in Israel[d] have I found such faith. 11 I tell you, many will come from east and west and recline at table with Abraham, Isaac, and Jacob in the kingdom of heaven, 12 while the sons of the kingdom will be thrown into the outer darkness. In that place there will be weeping and gnashing of teeth." 13 And to the centurion Jesus said, "Go; let it be done for you as you have believed." And the servant was healed at that very moment.

Jesus Calms a Storm

23 And when he got into the boat, his disciples followed him. 24 And behold, there arose a great storm on the sea, so that the boat was being swamped by the waves; but he was asleep. 25 And they went and woke him, saying, "Save us, Lord; we are perishing." 26 And he said to them, "Why are you afraid, O you of little faith?" Then he rose and rebuked the winds and the sea, and there was a great calm. 27 And the men marveled, saying, "What sort of man is this, that even winds and sea obey him?"

_____
_____
_____
_____
_____

LESSON 4:
EXPERIENCING THE FULLNESS OF WISDOM—THE SUPERNATURAL

What do we learn from these two stories about how God's supernatural power is manifested in our lives? How do we apply this to our lives?

> **Read Matthew 9:18-31:**
>
> A Girl Restored to Life and a Woman Healed
> 18 While he was saying these things to them, behold, a ruler came in and knelt before him, saying, "My daughter has just died, but come and lay your hand on her, and she will live." 19 And Jesus rose and followed him, with his disciples. 20 And behold, a woman who had suffered from a discharge of blood for twelve years came up behind him and touched the fringe of his garment, 21 for she said to herself, "If I only touch his garment, I will be made well." 22 Jesus turned, and seeing her he said, "Take heart, daughter; your faith has made you well." And instantly[a] the woman was made well. 23 And when Jesus came to the ruler's house and saw the flute players and the crowd making a commotion, 24 he said, "Go away, for the girl is not dead but sleeping." And they laughed at him. 25 But when the crowd had been put outside, he went in and took her by the hand, and the girl arose. 26 And the report of this went through all that district.
>
> Jesus Heals Two Blind Men
> 27 And as Jesus passed on from there, two blind men followed him, crying aloud, "Have mercy on us, Son of David." 28 When he entered the house, the blind men came to him, and Jesus said to them, "Do you believe that I am able to do this?" They said to him, "Yes, Lord." 29 Then he touched their eyes, saying, "According to your faith be it done to you." 30 And their eyes were opened. And Jesus sternly warned them, "See that no one knows about it." 31 But they went away and spread his fame through all that district.

_____
_____
_____
_____
_____

LESSON 4:
EXPERIENCING THE FULLNESS OF WISDOM—THE SUPERNATURAL

What does this reveal to us about the truth of the Hem of His Garment? What does this mean spiritually to us?

> **Read Numbers 15:37-41:**
>
> Tassels on Garments
> ³⁷ The Lord said to Moses, ³⁸ "Speak to the people of Israel, and tell them to make tassels on the corners of their garments throughout their generations, and to put a cord of blue on the tassel of each corner. ³⁹ And it shall be a tassel for you to look at and remember all the commandments of the Lord, to do them, not to follow[a] after your own heart and your own eyes, which you are inclined to whore after. ⁴⁰ So you shall remember and do all my commandments, and be holy to your God. ⁴¹ I am the Lord your God, who brought you out of the land of Egypt to be your God: I am the Lord your God."

_____
_____
_____
_____

What do these verses say are resident in His wings (Hem of His garment)? What does this then mean about healing and pursuing the Hem of His garment?

> **Read Malachi 4:2-3:**
>
> ² But for you who fear my name, the sun of righteousness shall rise with healing in its wings. You shall go out leaping like calves from the stall. ³ And you shall tread down the wicked, for they will be ashes under the soles of your feet, on the day when I act, says the Lord of hosts.

LESSON 4:
EXPERIENCING THE FULLNESS OF WISDOM—THE SUPERNATURAL

_____
_____
_____
_____
_____

As above, what do these verses say are resident in His wings (Hem of His garment)? What does this then mean about healing and pursuing the Hem of His garment?

> **Read Psalm 36:5-12:**
>
> ⁵ Your steadfast love, O Lord, extends to the heavens,
>   your faithfulness to the clouds.
> ⁶ Your righteousness is like the mountains of God;
>   your judgments are like the great deep;
>   man and beast you save, O Lord.
> ⁷ How precious is your steadfast love, O God!
>   The children of mankind take refuge in the shadow of your wings.
> ⁸ They feast on the abundance of your house,
>   and you give them drink from the river of your delights.
> ⁹ For with you is the fountain of life;
>   in your light do we see light.
> ¹⁰ Oh, continue your steadfast love to those who know you,
>   and your righteousness to the upright of heart!
> ¹¹ Let not the foot of arrogance come upon me,
>   nor the hand of the wicked drive me away.
> ¹² There the evildoers lie fallen;
>   they are thrust down, unable to rise.

_____
_____
_____
_____

LESSON 4:
EXPERIENCING THE FULLNESS OF WISDOM—THE SUPERNATURAL

What do these verses say about our experiencing God's supernatural work in our lives?

> **Read Acts 1:5-8:**
>
> 5 for John baptized with water, but you will be baptized with[a] the Holy Spirit not many days from now."
>
> The Ascension
> 6 So when they had come together, they asked him, "Lord, will you at this time restore the kingdom to Israel?" 7 He said to them, "It is not for you to know times or seasons that the Father has fixed by his own authority. 8 But you will receive power when the Holy Spirit has come upon you, and you will be my witnesses in Jerusalem and in all Judea and Samaria, and to the end of the earth."

_____
_____
_____
_____
_____

What happened at Pentecost that demonstrated His power of being a witness? How will this work on our lives?

> **Read Acts 2:1-4; 22:**
>
> The Coming of the Holy Spirit
> 2 When the day of Pentecost arrived, they were all together in one place. 2 And suddenly there came from heaven a sound like a mighty rushing wind, and it filled the entire house where they were sitting. 3 And divided tongues as of fire appeared to them and rested[a] on each one of them. 4 And they were all filled with the Holy Spirit and began to speak in other tongues as the Spirit gave them utterance.

LESSON 4:
EXPERIENCING THE FULLNESS OF WISDOM—THE SUPERNATURAL

> ²² "Men of Israel, hear these words: Jesus of Nazareth, a man attested to you by God with mighty works and wonders and signs that God did through him in your midst, as you yourselves know—

_____
_____
_____
_____

What happened for all the people who said yes to Peter and began to gather and receive the life, the wisdom of Christ? How does this apply to us?

> **Read Acts 2:40-47:**
>
> ⁴⁰ And with many other words he bore witness and continued to exhort them, saying, "Save yourselves from this crooked generation." ⁴¹ So those who received his word were baptized, and there were added that day about three thousand souls.
>
> The Fellowship of the Believers
> ⁴² And they devoted themselves to the apostles' teaching and the fellowship, to the breaking of bread and the prayers. ⁴³ And awe[a] came upon every soul, and many wonders and signs were being done through the apostles. ⁴⁴ And all who believed were together and had all things in common. ⁴⁵ And they were selling their possessions and belongings and distributing the proceeds to all, as any had need. ⁴⁶ And day by day, attending the temple together and breaking bread in their homes, they received their food with glad and generous hearts, ⁴⁷ praising God and having favor with all the people. And the Lord added to their number day by day those who were being saved.

LESSON 4:
EXPERIENCING THE FULLNESS OF WISDOM—THE SUPERNATURAL

> **Read Acts 3:1-10; 16:**
>
> The Lame Beggar Healed
>
> **3** Now Peter and John were going up to the temple at the hour of prayer, the ninth hour.[a] 2 And a man lame from birth was being carried, whom they laid daily at the gate of the temple that is called the Beautiful Gate to ask alms of those entering the temple. 3 Seeing Peter and John about to go into the temple, he asked to receive alms. 4 And Peter directed his gaze at him, as did John, and said, "Look at us." 5 And he fixed his attention on them, expecting to receive something from them. 6 But Peter said, "I have no silver and gold, but what I do have I give to you. In the name of Jesus Christ of Nazareth, rise up and walk!" 7 And he took him by the right hand and raised him up, and immediately his feet and ankles were made strong. 8 And leaping up, he stood and began to walk, and entered the temple with them, walking and leaping and praising God. 9 And all the people saw him walking and praising God, 10 and recognized him as the one who sat at the Beautiful Gate of the temple, asking for alms. And they were filled with wonder and amazement at what had happened to him.
>
> 16 And his name—by faith in his name—has made this man strong whom you see and know, and the faith that is through Jesus[a] has given the man this perfect health in the presence of you all.

LESSON 4:
EXPERIENCING THE FULLNESS OF WISDOM—THE SUPERNATURAL

In this story, how does God work in the lives of both Saul and Ananias? What does this teach us about wisdom and how we apply this in our lives?

Read Acts 9:1-19:

The Conversion of Saul
9 But Saul, still breathing threats and murder against the disciples of the Lord, went to the high priest [2] and asked him for letters to the synagogues at Damascus, so that if he found any belonging to the Way, men or women, he might bring them bound to Jerusalem. [3] Now as he went on his way, he approached Damascus, and suddenly a light from heaven shone around him. [4] And falling to the ground, he heard a voice saying to him, "Saul, Saul, why are you persecuting me?" [5] And he said, "Who are you, Lord?" And he said, "I am Jesus, whom you are persecuting. 6 But rise and enter the city, and you will be told what you are to do." [7] The men who were traveling with him stood speechless, hearing the voice but seeing no one. [8] Saul rose from the ground, and although his eyes were opened, he saw nothing. So they led him by the hand and brought him into Damascus. [9] And for three days he was without sight, and neither ate nor drank.

[10] Now there was a disciple at Damascus named Ananias. The Lord said to him in a vision, "Ananias." And he said, "Here I am, Lord." [11] And the Lord said to him, "Rise and go to the street called Straight, and at the house of Judas look for a man of Tarsus named Saul, for behold, he is praying, [12] and he has seen in a vision a man named Ananias come in and lay his hands on him so that he might regain his sight." [13] But Ananias answered, "Lord, I have heard from many about this man, how much evil he has done to your saints at Jerusalem. [14] And here he has authority from the chief priests to bind all who call on your name." [15] But the Lord said to him, "Go, for he is a chosen instrument of mine to carry my name before the Gentiles and kings and the children of Israel. [16] For I will show him how much he must suffer for the sake of my name." [17] So Ananias departed and entered the house. And laying his hands on him he said, "Brother Saul, the Lord Jesus who appeared to you on the road by which you came has sent me so that you may regain your sight and be filled with the Holy Spirit." [18] And immediately something like scales fell from his eyes, and he regained his sight. Then he rose and was baptized; [19] and taking food, he was strengthened.

Saul Proclaims Jesus in Synagogues
For some days he was with the disciples at Damascus.

LESSON 4:
EXPERIENCING THE FULLNESS OF WISDOM—THE SUPERNATURAL

_____
_____
_____
_____
_____

How did God work both sides of this story and give wisdom to fulfill His bigger story? Why is this so important in our seeking wisdom and following Him?

> **Read Acts 10:8-38:**
>
> [8] and having related everything to them, he sent them to Joppa.
>
> Peter's Vision
> [9] The next day, as they were on their journey and approaching the city, Peter went up on the housetop about the sixth hour[a] to pray. [10] And he became hungry and wanted something to eat, but while they were preparing it, he fell into a trance [11] and saw the heavens opened and something like a great sheet descending, being let down by its four corners upon the earth. [12] In it were all kinds of animals and reptiles and birds of the air. [13] And there came a voice to him: "Rise, Peter; kill and eat." [14] But Peter said, "By no means, Lord; for I have never eaten anything that is common or unclean." [15] And the voice came to him again a second time, "What God has made clean, do not call common." [16] This happened three times, and the thing was taken up at once to heaven.
>
> [17] Now while Peter was inwardly perplexed as to what the vision that he had seen might mean, behold, the men who were sent by Cornelius, having made inquiry for Simon's house, stood at the gate [18] and called out to ask whether Simon who was called Peter was lodging there. [19] And while Peter was pondering the vision, the Spirit said to him, "Behold, three men are looking for you. [20] Rise and go down and accompany them without hesitation,[b] for I have sent them." [21] And Peter went down to the men and said, "I am the one you are looking for. What is the reason for your coming?" [22] And they said, "Cornelius, a centurion, an upright and God-fearing man, who is well spoken of by the whole Jewish nation, was directed by a holy angel to send for you to come to his house and to hear what you have to say." [23] So he invited them in to be his guests.

LESSON 4:
EXPERIENCING THE FULLNESS OF WISDOM—THE SUPERNATURAL

The next day he rose and went away with them, and some of the brothers from Joppa accompanied him. 24 And on the following day they entered Caesarea. Cornelius was expecting them and had called together his relatives and close friends. 25 When Peter entered, Cornelius met him and fell down at his feet and worshiped him. 26 But Peter lifted him up, saying, "Stand up; I too am a man." 27 And as he talked with him, he went in and found many persons gathered. 28 And he said to them, "You yourselves know how unlawful it is for a Jew to associate with or to visit anyone of another nation, but God has shown me that I should not call any person common or unclean. 29 So when I was sent for, I came without objection. I ask then why you sent for me."

30 And Cornelius said, "Four days ago, about this hour, I was praying in my house at the ninth hour,[c] and behold, a man stood before me in bright clothing 31 and said, 'Cornelius, your prayer has been heard and your alms have been remembered before God. 32 Send therefore to Joppa and ask for Simon who is called Peter. He is lodging in the house of Simon, a tanner, by the sea.' 33 So I sent for you at once, and you have been kind enough to come. Now therefore we are all here in the presence of God to hear all that you have been commanded by the Lord."

Gentiles Hear the Good News
34 So Peter opened his mouth and said: "Truly I understand that God shows no partiality, 35 but in every nation anyone who fears him and does what is right is acceptable to him. 36 As for the word that he sent to Israel, preaching good news of peace through Jesus Christ (he is Lord of all), 37 you yourselves know what happened throughout all Judea, beginning from Galilee after the baptism that John proclaimed: 38 how God anointed Jesus of Nazareth with the Holy Spirit and with power. He went about doing good and healing all who were oppressed by the devil, for God was with him.

_____
_____
_____
_____
_____

LESSON 4:
EXPERIENCING THE FULLNESS OF WISDOM—THE SUPERNATURAL

What do these verses speak to how we play an important role in exercising God's supernatural work? What can we thus expect in our lives?

> **Read Luke 9:1-6; 10:17-20:**
>
> Jesus Sends Out the Twelve Apostles
> **9** And he called the twelve together and gave them power and authority over all demons and to cure diseases, ² and he sent them out to proclaim the kingdom of God and to heal. ³ And he said to them, "Take nothing for your journey, no staff, nor bag, nor bread, nor money; and do not have two tunics.[a] ⁴ And whatever house you enter, stay there, and from there depart. ⁵ And wherever they do not receive you, when you leave that town shake off the dust from your feet as a testimony against them." 6 And they departed and went through the villages, preaching the gospel and healing everywhere.
>
> The Return of the Seventy-Two
> ¹⁷ The seventy-two returned with joy, saying, "Lord, even the demons are subject to us in your name!" ¹⁸ And he said to them, "I saw Satan fall like lightning from heaven. ¹⁹ Behold, I have given you authority to tread on serpents and scorpions, and over all the power of the enemy, and nothing shall hurt you. ²⁰ Nevertheless, do not rejoice in this, that the spirits are subject to you, but rejoice that your names are written in heaven."

_____
_____
_____
_____
_____

LESSON 4:
EXPERIENCING THE FULLNESS OF WISDOM—THE SUPERNATURAL

What is the role of unity in experiencing the supernatural? How does this work in our everyday lives?

> **Read Matthew 18:18-20:**
>
> **18** Truly, I say to you, whatever you bind on earth shall be bound in heaven, and whatever you loose on earth shall be loosed[a] in heaven. **19** Again I say to you, if two of you agree on earth about anything they ask, it will be done for them by my Father in heaven. **20** For where two or three are gathered in my name, there am I among them."

_____
_____
_____
_____

> **Read Psalm 133:**
>
> When Brothers Dwell in Unity
> A Song of Ascents. Of David.
>
> **133** Behold, how good and pleasant it is
>   when brothers dwell in unity![a]
> **2** It is like the precious oil on the head,
>   running down on the beard,
> on the beard of Aaron,
>   running down on the collar of his robes!
> **3** It is like the dew of Hermon,
>   which falls on the mountains of Zion!
> For there the Lord has commanded the blessing,
>   life forevermore.

LESSON 4:
EXPERIENCING THE FULLNESS OF WISDOM—THE SUPERNATURAL

_____
_____
_____
_____
_____

As we reach unity and understand authority in that unity, how are we to pray? What does that mean to us personally?

> **Read Mark 11:20-25:**
>
> The Lesson from the Withered Fig Tree
> 20 As they passed by in the morning, they saw the fig tree withered away to its roots. 21 And Peter remembered and said to him, "Rabbi, look! The fig tree that you cursed has withered." 22 And Jesus answered them, "Have faith in God. 23 Truly, I say to you, whoever says to this mountain, 'Be taken up and thrown into the sea,' and does not doubt in his heart, but believes that what he says will come to pass, it will be done for him. 24 Therefore I tell you, whatever you ask in prayer, believe that you have received[a] it, and it will be yours. 25 And whenever you stand praying, forgive, if you have anything against anyone, so that your Father also who is in heaven may forgive you your trespasses."[b]

_____
_____
_____
_____
_____

Write in journal: As you pray for wisdom for the questions or unresolved issues for which you seek wisdom, what are you hearing? What prophetic word is God giving you? What supernatural work of God is required to fulfill the answer to your question or issue?

www.ingramcontent.com/pod-product-compliance
Lightning Source LLC
Chambersburg PA
CBHW051258110526
44589CB00025B/2876